Crazy Painting

Crazy Painting

Juliet Bawden

Designed by Jane Laycock
Illustrated by Jane Laycock
and Shelagh McGee

Beaver Books

For Caroline, Huw and Robin Phillips,
with love

A Beaver Book
Published by Arrow Books Limited
62-5 Chandos Place, London WC2N 4NW
An imprint of Century Hutchinson Ltd

London Melbourne Sydney Auckland
Johannesburg and agencies throughout the world

First published 1988
Reprinted 1989

Text © Juliet Bawden 1988
Illustrations © Century Hutchinson 1988

Set in Times by Book Ens, Saffron Walden, Essex

Made and printed in Great Britain
by The Guernsey Press Co. Ltd,
Guernsey, Channel Islands

ISBN 0 09 954320 6

Contents

5

Introduction

Crazy Painting is full of painting and decorating ideas. It tells you how to make your own paint and other materials, and how to create many different kinds of painting effects. Many of the materials you will need are made from household ingredients or cost only a few pennies, so you should have no difficulty getting started.

The dots at the beginning of each project show how easy it is. One dot means it is very easy, two dots mean it is a little more difficult, and three dots mean that you will have to concentrate really hard! It's probably a good idea to start with the easy projects and gradually work your way through to the hard ones. If in doubt ask a grown-up to help with the more difficult projects.

Have lots of fun painting!

Before you Begin

Types of Paint

For painting on paper or card watercolour and poster paints are best and easiest to use. You'll find a recipe for watercolour paint on p. 14. You can buy non-toxic poster paint, which is ideal for painting your face (see p. 61).

If you want a more textured effect, make some finger paint (see p. 15) and use that instead. Oil colours can be exciting to experiment with, too, and you'll need them to create a marbled pattern (see p. 41). You can buy them from any art shop, along with acrylic paints, which are useful for providing a strong base (see p. 87).

Crayons and felt-tip pens are also handy, and great fun to use. Try outlining shapes with them, or combining them with watercolours.

For stencilling why not try using metallic spray paints (see pp. 23 and 50). Spray paints should not be used in confined spaces, though, so, if possible, work outside when using them.

You can buy special paints for painting on glazed ceramics. Pebeo make a range of solvent-based paints called ceramic à froid for this purpose. These paints require no special fixing, but they do need to be left for at least twenty-four hours to dry. Once the paint is dry, you can varnish on top for extra protection.

Ceramic paints are best used on decorative rather than everyday objects. Wash by hand in warm, soapy water ceramics that you have painted. Never put them in a dishwasher.

Ceramic and stained glass paints by Pebeo are also suitable for marbling (see p. 41); while gloss paint, enamel paint (Deka colour) and ceramic à froid are all suitable for painting on enamelwear (see pp. 85, 87 and 89).

If you fancy dyeing fabrics, you can either use natural ingredients (see pp. 18 and 48), or a cold-water dye and fixative. Dylon make a wide range of these, which are essential for tie dyeing (see p. 107).

You can buy felt-tip pens especially for use on fabrics (see pp. 96 and 98). Pebeo and Pelikan both make a range of these, which you can buy individually or in sets. You can use pastel dye sticks on fabrics, too (see p. 105). These look just like wax crayons, and you can buy them in boxes of seven and fifteen different colours by Pentel.

Fabric paints are also available (see p. 99). You might like to try using glitter paint on a tee-shirt or sweat shirt (see p. 101). Both Dryad and Pebeo make this sort of paint, which can be used on fabrics, paper, leather, plastic, glass, and acetate. Pebeo also make a paint called 'Brod Express' that sits, puffed up, on the surface of fabric. You can make excellent squiggles with it (see p. 103).

Painting Tools

You'll need a range of paintbrushes, from those with very fine bristles for painting outlines, to those with thick bristles for filling in large shapes.

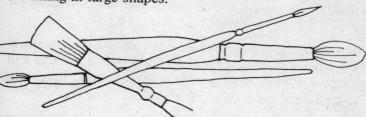

A giant, home-made ballpoint pen is ideal for filling in shapes, too. Make your own by following these instructions

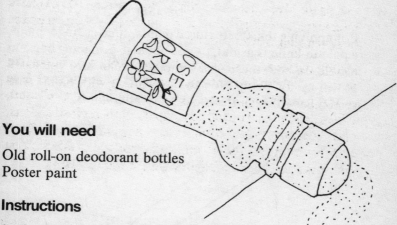

You will need

Old roll-on deodorant bottles
Poster paint

Instructions

1. Remove the ball top from the bottle.

2. Rinse out the bottle well.

3. Fill with poster paint, and push the ball back on.

11

For special painting effects you'll need some special tools. A sponge is a must for sponging (see p. 36), and useful for stencilling (see p. 50), if you don't have a stencil brush, which is also handy for spattering (see p. 38). An old toothbrush is good for spattering, too (see p. 38).

Sponge

Old toothbrush

Stencil brush →

For applying thicker, textured paints, such as finger paint, a palette-knife is useful, or you could use an icing bag and nozzle. In both these cases, though, make sure you ask a grown-up for permission to cover them with paint. And remember to wash them carefully afterwards.

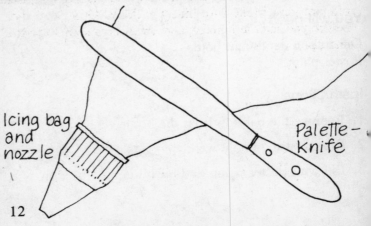

Icing bag and nozzle

Palette-knife

Helpful Hints

1. Always collect all your tools and materials before starting on a project. This includes turpentine substitute or white spirit if using oil- or solvent-based paint, cloth for wiping your hands, paper, fabric, inks, pens, and water for cleaning your brushes.

2. Spread lots of newspaper around your work area to prevent surfaces from becoming covered in paint, and to give yourself plenty of room to dry your projects.

3. Always cover yourself so that you do not spatter your clothes with paint. An apron will do, but better still try to beg an old shirt from a grown-up that will cover you from head to toe. Roll up the sleeves and, if it is too long, hitch it up with an old belt or a piece of string.

4. It is a good idea to keep the same kind of paints, pens, and inks together. Old tins, shoe boxes and trays are ideal for paints, inks, and dyes. If you can afford it, a plastic cutlery drawer is a good idea for keeping pens and crayons. The best way of storing brushes is to put them in old jam jars. Make sure that you ALWAYS clean them before you put them away, and always place them bristle-end up.

Making your own Materials ⌒

Watercolour and finger paints are easy to make, so why not have a go at making them yourself? While you're at it, you might like to try your hand at some bakers' clay or home-made charcoal. Follow the instructions carefully.

● Watercolour Paint

You will need

1 teaspoon detergent
1 teaspoon water
Capful food colouring
Bowl
Teaspoon

Instructions

1. With a teaspoon, stir all the ingredients together in a small bowl or jam jar.

2. In a separate bowl mix a different food colouring with detergent and water.

Ideas

To make more unusual colours, mix together small amounts of different-coloured home-made paint on a saucer.

14

● Finger Paint – 1

Finger paint is simply paint that has been thickened or textured. There are several different ways of making finger paint – this is the easiest.

You will need

Wallpaper paste
Old washing-up liquid bottles
Dry powder paint
Metal spoon

Instructions

1. Mix the wallpaper paste according to the instructions on the packet.

2. Pour the mixture into the bottles.

3. Squeeze the paste on to a plate and mix in the dry paint with a metal spoon.

● Finger Paint – 2

You will need

½ cup water
1 cup soap powder
Capful food colouring *or* powder paint
Metal spoon

Instructions

Mix all the ingredients together with a metal spoon.
The more colour you add, the richer-looking it will be.

●● Finger Paint – 3

You may need a grown-up around
when making this type of finger
paint, as it involves cooking.

You will need

1 cup cornflour
Enough water to dissolve it
Saucepan
1 litre boiling water
Wooden spoon
1 cup soap flakes
Powder paint *or* food colouring
Old margarine tubs
Metal spoon

Instructions

1. Place the cornflour in the saucepan and dissolve over a
low heat.

2. Add the boiling water to the dissolved cornflour.

3. With a wooden spoon, stir over the heat until the mixture thickens.

4. Remove from the heat and add the soap flakes.

5. Leave to cool.

6. Pour the mixture into tubs and, with a metal spoon, mix a different-coloured paint or food colouring in each.

● Natural Dyes

You can make dyes from many
natural substances, such as fruit,
vegetables, twigs, and herbs.

Some natural dyes and their colours

Tea – browns, khaki, and gingers (depending on the sort of
tea). You can use old tea left in the pot if you wish, or
new teabags.

Coffee – dark cream to dull gold. You can use old
coffee grounds.

Curry powder – dull creams and pale gold.

Onion skin – a range of colours, from orange to green.

Red cabbage – a wide range of colours, from pale rose to
lilacs. Use the oldest outer leaves of the cabbage.

Instructions

For instructions for dyeing please turn to page 48.

●● Invisible Ink

Here is a good way of sending secret messages! You may like to ask a grown-up to light the candle.

You will need

Juice of 1 lemon
Cup *or* small jar
Fine paintbrush
Paper
Matches
Iron *or* candle in a holder

Instructions

1. Make sure your paintbrush is clean.

2. Squeeze the lemon juice into the cup or jar.

3. Dip your paintbrush in the juice, and write your secret message. Leave it to dry. This will take only a few minutes.

4. Press down on the message with a hot iron to turn the letters brown. Or ask a grown-up to light the candle. Hold the paper close to it to read the message. When heated the lemon juice combines with oxygen and turns dark brown.

● Charcoal

Charcoal is good for drawing with.
You can make your own charcoal
by burning the end of a piece of
wood in a bonfire. Use the
blackened end to draw with.

● Glue

You will need

1 cup flour
2 cups water
Bowl
Fork

Instructions

Using a fork, mix the flour and water together in a bow
until smooth.

20

●● Bakers' Clay or Bread Dough

Although bakers' clay is sometimes known as bread dough it is inedible because of the large amount of salt included in the mixture and the extreme hardness to which it is baked.

It is a very good substitute for clay, and you can use it to make small models, picture frames, Christmas tree decorations, and model flowers and fruit to name just a few ideas. Then you can have fun painting and decorating them.

You will need

3 cups plain flour
Sieve
1 cup salt
1 teaspoon glycerine (this is not essential but it makes the clay easier to work with – buy it from the chemist)
1 cup water (the size of the cup is unimportant as long as the same cup is used for all the ingredients)

Instructions

1. Sieve the dry ingredients into a bowl, and add the glycerine.

2. Pour in the water, stirring continuously.

3. Continue stirring until the mixture is fairly stiff. Take it out of the bowl and knead it like bread. If it is too dry, add

more water. If it is too wet, add more flour. (If you do not wish to use it immediately, wrap the clay in cling film or place in an airtight plastic container and store in a cool place for a few days.)

4. Cut into shapes. If you are making tree decorations, use fancy pastry cutters to make your shapes, and don't forget to make a hole near the top of the shape so that you can hang it.

5. Place on a baking tray and bake at about 180°C. The length of time it takes to cook will depend on how large and how thick the shapes are. Ask a grown-up to check when the dough is hard, and remove from the oven.

6. When the dough is cool you can begin painting.

22

●●● Cutting a Stencil

Stencils were first made in western China in the tenth century. They started to be used in Europe in the fifteenth century. Some of the prettiest examples of stencilwork can be found in the artefacts of the eighteenth-century American colonists. They used stencils to decorate floors, walls and bed coverings, taking their inspiration from nature; willows, oak leaves, fruit, and eagles were especially popular.

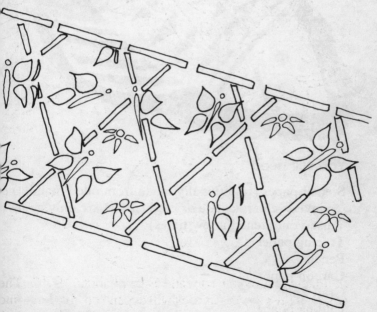

When designing stencils remember to incorporate lots of 'bridges'. Bridges are the parts which hold the design together. Basketwork, trelliswork, fish scales, skeletons, fruit, flowers, birds, ice-cream cornets, and cones are all ideal for stencil design.

You will need

Stencil paper (traditionally made from oiled manilla) *or* vinyl *or* clear acetate *or* card (if you are only going to use your stencil a few times)
Tracing paper
Pencil
Carbon paper
Craft knife
Cutting board
Sheets thick paper
Masking tape
Black felt-tip pen

Instructions

1. Trace the ice-cream and cone design from page 26 on to tracing paper.

2. Place a piece of carbon paper, face-down, between the tracing paper and the stencil paper. Make sure that you leave a border of at least 5 cm. around your design.

3. Go over the design again with a pen. Remove the tracing paper and carbon paper and define the design left on the stencil paper more strongly with a black felt-tip pen.

4. Place the stencil paper, with the design uppermost, on a cutting board made of chipboard plywood or block-board. Fix it in place with masking tape.

5. Using a craft knife cut the straight edges with a firm, fluent movement.

6. Remove the masking tape and cut round the curves: it is easier to do this if you move the paper and keep the knife still.

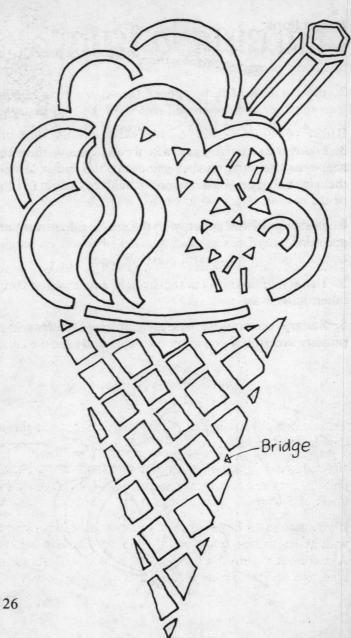

Bridge

Learning to Paint

Before you start painting an outer space mural on your bedroom wall, it's a good idea to get used to drawing shapes and patterns, and using fine and thick brushes to fill them in. You'll need to know something about colour, too, or the overall effect could be disgusting!

Colours are divided into two categories: primary colours and secondary colours.

There are three primary colours: RED, BLUE, and YELLOW. These colours cannot be made by mixing other colours together.

Secondary colours are made by mixing together two primary colours. So:

Yellow + blue = green
Blue + red = purple
Red + yellow = orange

To make a colour lighter simply add white; to make it darker add black.

If you have only a limited amount of money to purchase paint or printing ink, then buy the primary colours plus black and white.

If you can buy a large range of paint colours experiment with them to see what weird colours you can make. Always begin with the lightest colour you wish to combine, and add the darker colours to it. Try adding them in different amounts, and make a note of what you do, so you can make the same colour again if you like it.

You'll find in this section all the techniques you need to know to do every single project in the book. Don't worry about learning them all now. Concentrate on painting shapes and making patterns. You can come back to sponging or stencilling later when you've done some of the easy projects.

● Painting Shapes and Patterns

Abstract shapes are great for making patterns. Here are a few ideas for you to copy or trace, and colour in.

Use a pencil or felt-tip pen to draw the outline, then fill in the shape with felt-tips or watercolour paints. Use a ruler to draw straight lines, and try to buff up to the edges neatly. This is easiest with a fine-bristled brush; save the coarser, thicker brushes for large expanses.

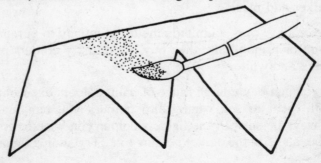

Try drawing some shapes of your own. Here are some ideas that might come in useful.

Use other objects to draw round, too. Plates are ideal for circles and to help you shape a large, billowy cloud. Pastry cutters are good for many animal shapes.

Now choose some of the shapes you have drawn and copy them on to your paper so that they make a pattern. Some shapes fit together much better than others. Experiment until you feel confident about painting and drawing both curvy shapes and geometric shapes.

Of course, you don't have to fill in the shapes completely. If you want you can paint stripes or large dots in the middle of them. You can use more than one colour per shape, too, although you'll have to wait for the first coat of paint to dry before applying another on top. And you'll have to understand about colour.

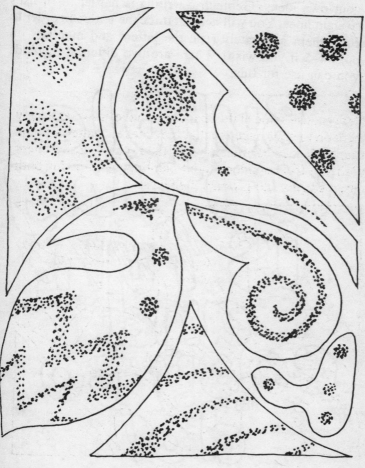

● Lettering

Bubble writing is fun and easy to do, as it uses curved lines which do not need to be drawn completely accurately. Just copy the shapes of the letters shown here, and then think of your own ideas. Geometric writing is harder, as it uses straight lines. You will need to trace the letters in order to copy them accurately (use the letters and numbers on pp. 34–5 if you wish). There are two different methods you can use for this.

Method 1

You will need

Tracing paper
Soft pencil (B or 2B)
Paper

Instructions

1. Place the tracing paper over the letters and go over all the lines carefully with your pencil.

2. Turn your tracing paper over, and go over all the lines again with your pencil.

3. Now turn your tracing over once again. Place it on top of your paper, and go over the tracing again with your pencil. The tracing will be transferred to your sheet of paper.

Method 2

You will need

Carbon paper
Pen
Paper

Instructions

1. Place the carbon paper on to your sheet of paper, ink side downwards.

2. Place the sheet of letters that you wish to trace on top of the carbon paper.

3. Go over the lines of the letters carefully with your pen. You will find that the shapes of the letters have been transferred to your sheet of paper.

A B C D E F G

H I J K L M N

O P Q R S T U

V W X Y Z

abcdefghi
jklmnopq
rstuvwxyz
1234567890

● Sponging

For an interesting, mottled pattern that is different every time you try it apply several different-coloured paints, one by one, to a plain surface. Sponging is easy to do, if a bit messy!

You will need

Newspaper
Watercolour paints
Sponge
Bowl
Jam jar lids *or* saucers
Paper

Instructions

1. Cover the area where you are going to work with newspaper.

2. Mix some colours on jam jar lids or saucers to decide which combination of colours you like best. Choose three – one dark, one medium, and one pale.

3. Make up some of the darkest colour paint in a bowl.

4. Dip the sponge in the paint, being careful not to overload it.

5. Dab the sponge firmly on the paper. Space the colour widely and evenly over the paper. Leave to dry.

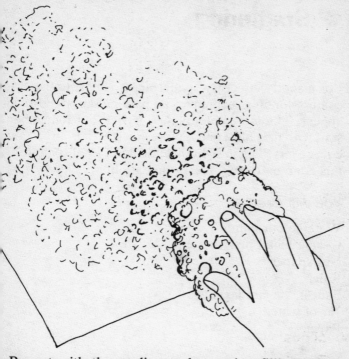

Repeat with the medium colour paint, filling in be-
~~~een and overlapping the darker colour. Leave to dry.

Soften the effect by adding the third, very pale, colour
~~ndomly over the other two colours. Leave to dry.

~eas

~y the same technique using oil paints thinned with white
~irit. Sponged paper makes marvellous wrapping paper,
~ paper for covering books. For a foggy look apply the
~cond coat of paint before the first coat is dry.

~ou can also sponge ceramics (see p. 90), and, of
~urse, walls.

● Spattering

For a spotty effect try spattering. It is best to use brigh
colours for this technique, as pale colours tend to di
appear. The more colours the merrier, but remember t
start with the palest one. Before you start it is important t
cover everything in sight that you don't want spattered, a
this is an extremely messy operation!

You will need

Watercolour paints
Coarse paintbrush *or* stencil brush
Newspaper
Ruler
Saucers *or* jam jar lids
Jar of water
Paper

Instructions

1. Cover the area where you are going to work wi
newspaper.

2. Mix some colours on jam jar lids or saucers to decic
which combination you like best. You can use any numb
of colours.

3. Dip your brush into the palest colour paint. Do n
overload it.

4. Hold the ruler over the bottom edge of the paper, a
strike the handle of the brush against it. Repeat until t
paper is covered with spots.

38

. Wash the brush and apply the next darkest colour in
the same way. Continue until you have used all your
chosen colours, or you have achieved the effect you want.
Leave to dry.

Ideas

Try using a toothbrush instead of a paintbrush. Dip the
toothbrush in the paint and run the ruler slowly along
the bristles.

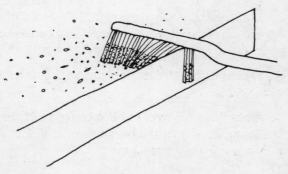

Try replacing watercolour paints with oil paints. Dilute them with white spirit to the consistency of milk before spattering.

You can also spatter ceramics (see p. 90), and fabrics (see p. 100).

● Marbling – 1

Marbling is one of the simplest
and most effective ways of
decorating a surface with pattern.
It is called marbling because the
wavy veined patterns look like
marble.

As you probably know, oil and water do not mix, and the
earliest method of marbling was to float oil colours on
water.

Here is an easy way of creating a marbled effect, using this
ancient technique, and materials that are readily available.

You will need

Watertight container (a square washing-up bowl, a
    photographic dish, *or* a roasting pan).
Oil- *or* solvent-based paints
White spirit
Turpentine substitute
Metal spoon
Paintbrush
Jars
Jam jar lids *or* saucers
Old newspaper
Cloth
Paper

Instructions

1. Cover the area where you are going to work with

newspaper. Spread enough newspaper to set your marbled paper while it is drying.

2. Fill the bowl with water.

3. Mix the paint with some white spirit until it is the consistency of thin cream.

4. Drop the runny paint on the water and swirl it around with the paintbrush handle.

5. Lay the paper gently on the surface of the water – the paint will stick to it.

6. Lift the paper off the water and turn it over so that the marbled surface is face-up. Leave it to dry on a sheet of newspaper.

7. Wipe your hands with turpentine substitute to remove the paint, before washing them in soap and water.

Ideas

Once dry, use your marbled paper for wrapping presents, or covering books. Or hang it on the wall as a work of art. You could also use it to cover boxes, cans, or jars to make desk tidies.

You can marble ceramic tiles, material, china and even candles.

●● Marbling – 2

This is very similar to the first method. However, the addition of wallpaper paste to the water gives you more control over the design.

You will need

Watertight container (a square washing-up bowl, a photographic dish, *or* a roasting pan)
1 litre water
1 dessertspoon wallpaper adhesive
Metal spoon
Oil- *or* solvent-based paints
White spirit
Turpentine substitute
Paintbrush
Jar
Jam jars, lids, *or* saucers
Lots of newspaper
Cloth
Paper

Instructions

1. Cover your working area with newspaper, leaving enough space to dry the marbled paper.

2. Mix the wallpaper paste and the water together, making sure that the paste dissolves completely. It will take about ten minutes for the water to become a jelly-like consistency.

3. In a jar or small jug, mix the paint with white spirit until it is the consistency of thin cream.

4. Pour the paint on to the water and paste mixture in a curved line.

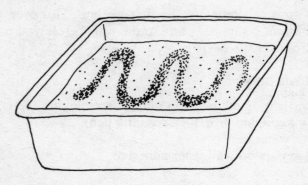

5. Pull the handle of the paintbrush through the paint to create a 'feather' effect.

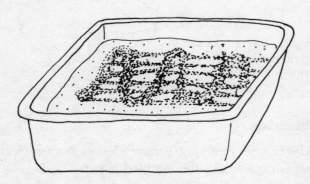

6. Lay your paper on top quickly, before the colours merge into one another.

7. Lift the paper quickly and leave to dry on newspaper, marbled-side-up.

●● Potato Printing

You will need

Newspaper
Potatoes
Small vegetable knife
Paper
Poster paint
Small plate *or* saucer
Felt-tip pen

Instructions

1. Wash and peel the potato. Cut it in half, making sure you have cut a flat surface.

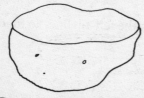 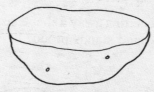

2. Draw a shape on the flat surface with a felt-tip pen.

3. Cut away the potato on the outside of the line with a small vegetable knife. The remaining shape stands proud of the rest of the potato. This is the part that will print.

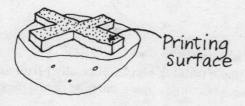

Printing Surface

45

4. On a piece of newspaper dab any surplus starch off the potato.

5. Pour the poster paint on to the plate or saucer.

6. Dip the potato into the paint so that the raised surface is completely covered with it.

7. Press the potato down firmly but gently on to the paper. Continue making the pattern.

8. Repeat for each colour, cutting different potato shapes.

NOTE: It is a good idea to use a different block of potato for each colour to stop the colours from going muddy.

You will have to make new blocks each day, as potatoes go soft if left overnight.

Ideas

Try cutting away a shape inside the felt-tip line, so that the surround stands proud.

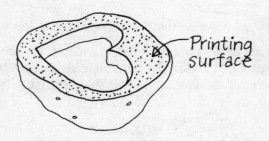

Printing surface

You can make printing blocks from other fruit and vegetables, such as onions, apples, carrots, pears, peppers, and

46

parsnips, which have their own built-in patterns when cut in half.

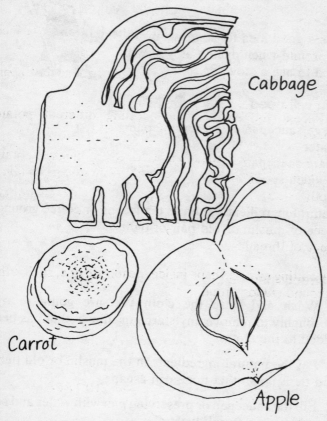

Cabbage

Carrot

Apple

You can carve patterns into plasticine to make printing blocks.

Almost anything with an interesting, raised surface can be used for printing: coins, dry biscuits, and leaves are all good. The rim of an egg cup will give you a circle, and Lego blocks will provide you with lots of dots.

47

●● Dyeing

It is a good idea for a grown-up to be around when dyeing as you will need to use a stove.

You will need

Large saucepan *or* preserving pan
Water
Spare saucepan
Wooden spoon
Cloth
Natural ingredients, such as tea leaves or coffee grounds
Piece of muslin *or* old pair of tights
Piece of thread

Instructions

1. Wash and rinse the cloth you are going to dye thoroughly to remove any starch or 'finish' that has been added to the cloth.

2. Put the natural ingredients in the muslin or old tights and tie it up so that none can escape.

3. Fill the saucepan or preserving pan with water and add the parcel of natural dyestuff.

4. Add the cloth and bring the water to the boil stirring all the time.

5. Turn the heat down and simmer. Occasionally and VERY CAREFULLY, lift the cloth out of the water with the spoon to check how the colour is doing.

6. When the colour is deep enough turn off the heat and very carefully remove the cloth and place it in the spare saucepan.

7. Rinse the cloth in cold water. Remove and leave to dry.

NOTE: It is easier to dye natural materials than man-made materials. Silk, cotton, and wool will all take dye more readily than nylon.

It is impossible to predict the results you will achieve each time you do some dyeing so dye all the yarn or fabric you wish to be the same colour in the same batch.

●●● Stencilling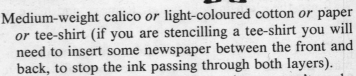

You will need

Medium-weight calico *or* light-coloured cotton *or* paper *or* tee-shirt (if you are stencilling a tee-shirt you will need to insert some newspaper between the front and back, to stop the ink passing through both layers).

Pots of paint (if you are using spray paint you won't need a brush or sponge) *or* fabric paint

Stencil brush (a hard-bristled stubby brush with flat ends) *or* sponge

Instructions

1. If you are printing on fabric, prepare it by washing out any dressing which may have been added. Dry and press, then cut it to the size you require.

2. Pin the paper or fabric to a piece of board – insulation board is ideal – or an old kitchen table.

3. Fix the outer edge of the stencil paper on to the fabric, paper or tee-shirt, using masking tape. (To cut your stencil see p. 23.)

4. Pour your paint on a saucer if you are brushing or sponging it on. If you are using a spray, make sure that everywhere that you don't want paint is covered with newspaper.

5. If you are using a stencil brush, make sure that it is dry. Hold it in an upright position and dip it in the paint.

6. Apply only small amounts of paint to the material you are stencilling or you will find that the paint bleeds under the edges of the stencil. Hold the stencil with one hand and the brush vertically with the other. Dab the paint on to the cloth or paper with an up and down motion.

7. Stamp off any surplus paint on to a sheet of newspaper.

8. Lift off the stencil. Wipe it clean with a damp cloth and hang it to dry.

9. Leave the stencilled paper to dry. If you have been stencilling fabric, hang the material up to dry. To fix it read the instructions on your paint container. Usually fixing is done by ironing on the back once your fabric is dry.

NOTE: If you wish to increase the strength of the colour gradually, start with the palest shade and build up to the darker tones.

For a well-blended effect, cover the entire design with a pale colour, then put a darker colour on the brush and continue dabbing.

Ideas

Use stencils to make wrapping-paper designs. Instead of using paint, use glue and then sprinkle the design with glitter.

Hats, Headbands and Specs ∿

● Magician's Cone Hat

You will need

Plate
Thin card *or* thick paper
Black, silver, and gold poster paints
Paintbrush
Elastic
Glue (Copydex is best)

Optional extras

Tissue
Crêpe paper
Tinsel
Beads
Pasta shapes

Instructions

1. Place a plate face-down on your card and draw around it. Remove the plate.

2. Draw a line across the centre of the circle and cut along it to make two semi-circles. (This will make two hats.)

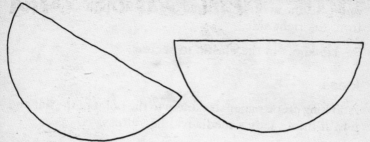

3. Paint one semi-circle black, and leave to dry.

4. Paint gold and silver moons and stars on the black background.

5. Apply glue all the way down the straight edge and stick together to make a cone shape. Hold it together while the glue dries.

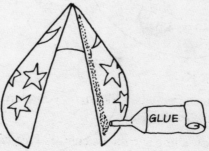

53

6. 1 cm from the bottom of the cone, make two holes opposite one another. Thread the elastic through the holes from the right side.

7. Tie knots in the elastic to secure.

Ideas

Add long crêpe paper streamers to the point of the hat and turn it into a lady's mediaeval headdress.

Make a Christmas tree hat by painting it green and sticking on tinsel and painted pasta bows.

Make a clown's hat by painting your cone a bright colour and sticking three different-coloured pom-poms on to the front.

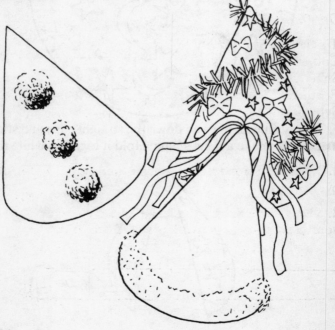

● Indian Brave Headband

Headbands are very easy to make
and you can experiment with some
exciting varieties.

You will need

Thin card *or* thick paper (brown wrapping paper is
    ideal)
Scissors
Glue (Copydex is best)
Paints and paintbrush *or* crayons

Optional extras

Tissue and crêpe paper
Cotton wool
Shiny sweet papers
Feathers
Sellotape

Instructions

1. Measure around your head and add 2 cm for
overlap.

2. Cut a piece of card the length of the circumference of
your head plus 2 cm overlap, and 5 cm deep.

↑5 cm

3. Paint geometric patterns the length of the headband and stick a feather in the middle.

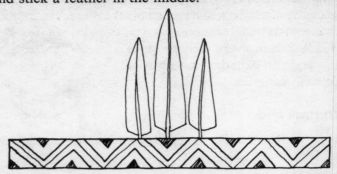

4. Apply glue to the underside of one end of the headband and stick the 2 cm overlap on top. Hold together for a few seconds until it is secure.

Ideas

Be a space alien: cut out a star and moon, paint them and stick them on the headband.

Be a May Queen: cover your headband in paper flowers. Cut out circles of tissue paper. Take hold of the centre of one, twist it firmly, and tie with cotton.

Make a pirate's hat by cutting the headband deeper —
about 13 cm. Shape the headband so that it is deepest at
the centre of the front and paint it black. When it is dry add
a white skull and crossbones at the deepest point.

Make a crown for a king by cutting a 13 cm-deep headband and cutting a serrated edge. Stick cotton wool round
the base of the crown, and add shiny shapes at intervals
around the centre of the band (sweet papers are good
for this).

Add hair to a headband for a Cleopatra look. Cut crepe paper into strips and stick it to the bottom of the headband.

Real hair

Crêpe paper

● Heart Specs

You will need

Elastic
Pencil
Thin card
Scissors
Paint and paintbrush *or* felt-tip pens

Optional extras

Glitter
Flowers

Instructions

1. Trace off the pattern shown on p. 60 on to card and cut out.

2. Paint little red hearts all over the specs.

3. Make holes in each side and thread the elastic through. Adjust to fit and tie knots to secure.

Ideas

Instead of heart-shaped glasses cut square, round or oval ones. Add glitter or flowers on top of the paint.

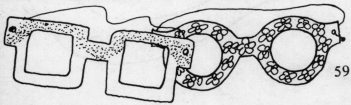

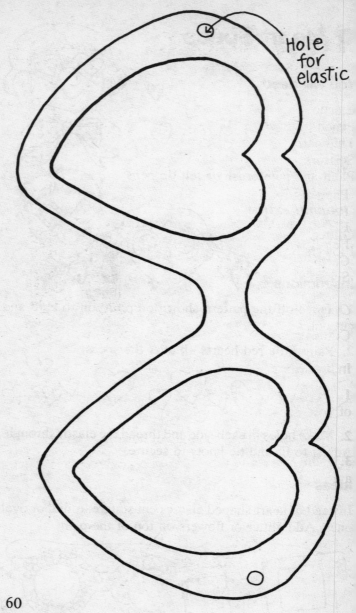

Hole
for
elastic

60

New Faces

● Clown Face

You will need

Paper plate
Pencil
Elastic
Felt-tip pens *or* watercolour paints
Card
Scissors

Optional extra

Cotton wool

Instructions

1. Put the plate in front of your face and mark the position of your eyes.

2. Take the plate away and cut out the eye holes.

3. Paint on a clown face. Make a big red mouth, a blob for a nose, and crosses around the eyes.

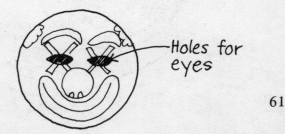

Holes for eyes

4. 1 cm in from the edge of the plate, make two small holes, one opposite the other. From the back of the mask thread the elastic through the holes.

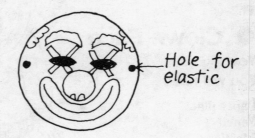

Hole for elastic

5. Adjust the elastic until it is the right length to go around your head. It should be tight but not so tight that it distorts the plate. Tie knots in the ends of the elastic.

Ideas

Try making the face of a lion or a witch.

●● Gruesome Features

This is a paper bag mask.
Never use a plastic bag.

You will need

Scissors
Large paper bag
Watercolour paints and paintbrush
Sellotape or glue

Optional extras

Thin card (such as an old tissue box or the sort a shirt is
    wrapped around)
Wool *or* cotton wool
Crêpe paper

Instructions

1. Put the paper bag over your head and with a pencil
mark the position of the eyes.

2. Remove the bag and cut out the eyes.

3. Paint the bag all over in the colour you wish the skin to
be – green if you want to look like a Martian. Leave to
dry.

4. Draw, then paint, some ferocious or outlandish features in eye-catching colours.

Ideas

Try making ears and noses out of thin card, painting them,

and then sticking them to your paper bag mask. For a tube nose, either use an old toilet roll tube or cut out a rectangle and stick the long sides together to make a tube. Or you could make a cone nose: cut out a circle and divide it in half in the same way as for a cone hat (see p. 52); stick the straight edge to itself to make a cone. Cut a serrated edge on the bottom of the nose and sides of the ears, where they will be glued to the mask. Make enormous elephant ears and paint them bright pink. Curl crepe paper and stick on top of the bag for hair. Or stick on cotton wool for a beard or hair and then paint it.

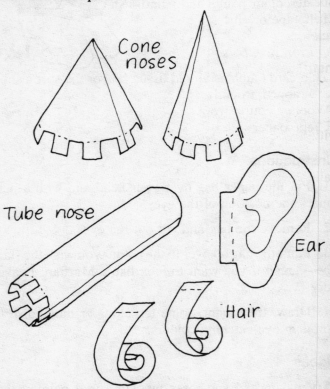

Cone noses

Tube nose

Ear

Hair

● ● Death Mask

You will need

Newspaper ripped into 2 cm-wide strips
Wallpaper paste
Round balloon
Paints and paintbrush
Vaseline
Bucket
Elastic
Scissors

Instructions

1. Blow up the balloon.

2. Dip your fingers in the vaseline and coat the balloon with it.

3. Soak strips of paper in the paste. Also cover the balloon with paste; standing it in a bucket as you work.

4. Cover the balloon with seven layers of paper, and then leave to dry.

65

5. Cut the balloon in half to make two masks.

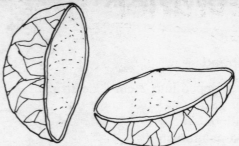

6. Coat one balloon mask with white paint, and leave to dry.

7. With black paint, paint on the features of a skull: huge black eye sockets, triangular black nose, and black gaps between the teeth. Try to paint black triangles beneath the cheek bones to give the skull a truly gaunt look.

8. 1 cm in from the edge of the balloon mask, make two small holes, one opposite the other. Thread the elastic through the holes from the back of the mask.

9. Tie knots in the ends of the elastic when you have adjusted it to the right length.

Ideas

Try making a ghost face.

Celebration Time

Cards, decorations, wrapping paper, invitations – all these you can make and paint yourself.

● Abstract Wrapping Paper

If you are very broke, why not make your own wrapping paper out of brown paper.

You will need

Brown paper
Pencil
Paints and paintbrush *or* felt-tip pens

Instructions

1. With a pencil draw bold wavy lines and squiggles all over the paper.

2. Colour them in with bright paints or felt-tip pens. Decorate some with dots and stripes.

Ideas

Wrap your present in newspaper. Continue the black-and white theme by making a big bow from either a white or a black bin liner. Write your message in big black felt-tip letters.

Make potato blocks (see p. 45) and print potato patterns on to paper.

Make marbled or sponged paper (see pp. 41 and 36).

Using a sponge or stencil brush, dab a pattern on to paper through a doily or stencil (see p. 50).

Cut out pictures from old cards and magazines and stick them on to paper to make collages.

Cover some paper with gummed paper shapes.

●● Christmas Banner

Is it someone's birthday or Christmas time? Make a big banner to celebrate.

You will need

Roll of lining paper *or* plain wallpaper (if you find some left-over wallpaper that isn't plain, use the back of it)
Pencil
Rubber
Ruler
Paints and paintbrush

Instructions

1. Outline in pencil the letters that make up the words 'Merry Christmas', using bubble writing (see p. 32). To get the spacing right, count the number of letters and add one for each space. MERRY CHRISTMAS has fourteen letters and three spaces: one at the beginning of MERRY, one between the two words, and one at the end of CHRISTMAS. So that's seventeen altogether.

2. Decide how long you want your banner to be and divide it by seventeen (the number of letters and spaces).

3. Using a ruler and pencil, divide the paper evenly into seventeen. This way you will know exactly where to place each letter and space.

4. Using a pencil draw the outline of each letter. Try to make each letter fill its space, from top to bottom, and from side to side.

5. When you have drawn out the letters neatly in pencil fill them in with paint. Try using two colours – red and green – for alternate letters. Then, if you're feeling really festive, paint two prickly holly leaves and some red berries in the space between the two words.

Ideas

Make a banner for a friend's birthday with 'Happy Birthday' painted on it, and balloons between the words.

●● Concertina Invitations

You will need

Thin card *or* thick paper, such as cartridge paper
Pencil
Pens *or* felt-tips
Paints and paintbrush
Scissors
Gingerbread man pastry cutter
Envelopes (if you haven't got any, why not make your own from paper?)

Instructions

1. Cut a strip of card to the height of your gingerbread man pastry cutter and four times as long.

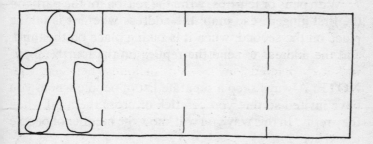

2. Fold the strip of card back and forth into four equal parts, so that it looks like a concertina.

3. Place the pastry cutter on top of the folded card and draw around it. The shape must touch the top edge of the concertina card.

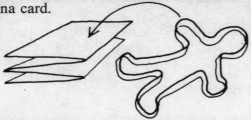

4. Cut around the shape through all the layers of card. Open it up: it should still be joined together by the hands.

5. Paint the gingerbread men light brown and leave to dry.

6. Paint on black eyes, noses and mouths. Leave to dry.

7. With pens or felt-tips, write the reason for the party on the first gingerbread man; the address where it is taking place on the second; when it is taking place on the third; and the address to send the replies on the fourth.

NOTE: Always keep a separate list of people whom you have invited so that you can tick or cross them off when they reply. In this way you will know the number of people to expect.

Ideas

Use other pastry cutters for differently shaped concertina invitations: try a house shape, a teapot or an animal.

●●● Pirate Party Decorations

Decorate paper plates, cups and tablecloth. Make your own place names, crackers, and food labels.

You will need

Black cloth
White tablecloth
Paper plates and cups
Thin card
Scissors
Chinagraph pencil *or* chalk
Drinking straws
Glue
Non-toxic felt-tip pens
Fabric paints and paintbrush
Brown paper bags

Instructions

1. Draw a parrot on each plate and colour them in with felt-tips.

2. On the tablecloth draw a blue ocean, blue sky, sun, seabirds, galleons, fish and treasure islands. Colour them in with felt-tips.

3. Cut the black cloth into rectangles, and draw a skull and crossbones on each with a chinagraph pencil or chalk.

Paint the skull and crossbones with white fabric paint. Leave to dry.

Apply glue to the edge of each rectangle of cloth, and wrap each one round a drinking straw.

Draw skull and crossbones on the brown paper bags and write the word 'SWAG' in black felt-tip underneath them in bubble writing (see p. 32). Put going-home presents in them.

Make cone hats in the same way as the magician's hat p. 52. Paint the card black before glueing it together. Afterwards paint on the skull and crossbones with white paint.

eas

incess and frog party:

raw pretty ribbons all over the plates and tablecloth.

Make tissue-paper flowers (see p. 56) and stick on the

edge of the tablecloth. Draw frogs on the cups and plate
Make mediaeval princess cone hats (see p. 54).

Circus party:

Draw different clown faces on the plates. Make big fe
from card and stick to the bottom of the cups. Make clow
cone hats (see p. 54). Draw brightly coloured streame
on the tablecloth. Draw round the flower shape on p. 7
and write your name in the centre. Sellotape a safety-p
to the back to make a badge.

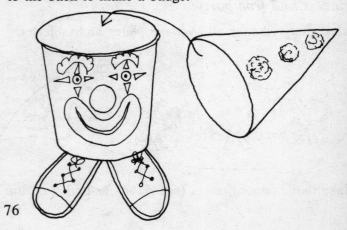

76

Monster party:

Paint large footprints all over the tablecloth. Draw the weirdest and ugliest faces you can on the plates. Cut monstrous arms and legs out of card and stick on to the cups. Make monster badges from card.

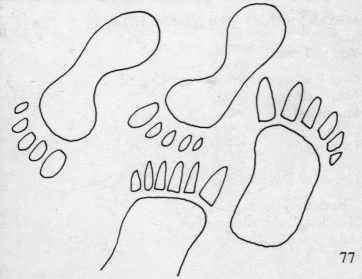

The Body Beautiful

●● Harlequin Face

Before you cover yourself from head to toe in a strange paint check that you are not allergic to it by doing a test patch of your mixture on the inside of your elbow. If it feels sore or goes the slightest bit red, do not paint your skin with it.

Do not use this paint near your eyes or mouth.

You can also use charcoal for painting yourself. If you want to make your own, burn one end of a piece of wood (see p. 20).

Mud also makes a good paint for bodies.

You will need

Cold cream *or* vaseline *or* cooking oil
Non-toxic poster paint
Paintbrushes
Saucers
Little water

Optional extras

2 pairs thick tights
Needle and thread
Bells

78

Instructions

1. Cover the part of you that you wish to paint in either cold cream, vaseline or oil. This will enable you to wash off the paint easily and prevent the paint from staining your skin. It will also give a glossy finish.

2. Mix the paint on the saucers with a little water.

3. With the aid of a mirror paint one side of your face black and one side white.

4. When the base paint is dry, paint on bright red and green diamonds. Make sure to keep the pattern perfectly symmetrical.

5. Wrap the tights round and round each other to make a messy hat, and glue together.

6. Draw a line down the middle, and paint one half black and the other white (the other way round to your face).

7. Sew bells on to the tights.

Ideas

Copy tattoo designs, such as butterflies, bluebirds, ships, and mermaids. Draw a clown's face, or the face of an animal, such as a tiger, rabbit, cat or dog. Draw on wrinkles, and age by sixty years.

Use flour or talcum powder to turn your hair grey or white.

Make lumpy, bumpy skin by sticking soggy cornflakes, bits of bread and Rice Krispies on to your skin with syrup or honey!

●●● Papier Mâché Jewellery

You will need

Thin card (old tissue boxes, the card
  included with folded shirts)
Tissues
Wallpaper paste *or* flour and water mixed to a thick cream
  paste (3 parts flour, 2 parts water) with a few drops of
  cloves added to preserve it (available from chemists)
Metal spoon
Newspaper cut or ripped into 5 mm-wide strips
White poster *or* acrylic paint
Poster paints *or* designers' gouache
Paintbrushes
Clear varnish (nail varnish will do)
Brooch backs *or* earring backs
Strong glue
Scissors

Instructions

1. Following the instructions on the packet, mix the
wallpaper paste with a metal spoon. Alternatively, make a
stiff paste out of flour and water.

2. Copy or trace some simple shapes, such as the ones
shown on p. 81, on to your card. Cut these out.

3. Rip a tissue into small pieces. Then crumple the tissue
pieces up and dip them into the paste. Stick them in the
middle of the shapes you have cut out to make them 3-D.

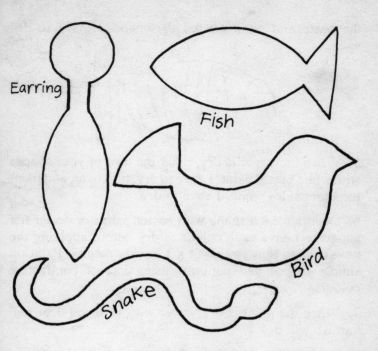

Leave to dry. To speed up the drying, place on a piece of paper on top of a radiator.

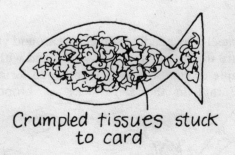

Crumpled tissues stuck
to card

4. When the tissue paper is dry, dip strips of newspaper in the paste and wrap around the shapes. Leave to dry again.

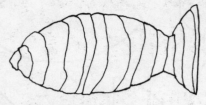

5. When the paper is dry, paint the tops of your shapes with white poster paint. Leave to dry, turn over, and paint the other sides white. Leave to dry.

6. Decorate each shape with poster paints or designers' gouache. Leave each colour to dry before applying the next one, so that you don't get muddy results. Paint on simple shapes and patterns, using lots of contrasting colours.

7. When the paint is dry, cover with varnish (clear nail varnish will do).

8. Stick the brooch or earring backs to the backs of your papier mâché shapes to complete your brooches or earrings.

Ideas

Make a bracelet by bending some card around your wrist, making sure that it will slip over your hand with room to spare. Staple or stick the ends together to form a circle. Then decorate in the same way as brooches and earrings.

Bottles, Boxes, Mugs and Plates

● Colourful Bottles

Metallic spray paint should not be used in a confined space. So, if possible, work outside (but not on a windy day).

You will need

Old milk bottles, wine bottles *or* jam jars
Metallic car spray paints
Masking tape
Newspaper
Scissors

Instructions

1. Spread newspaper all over the area in which you are working.

2. Cut shapes out of masking tape and stick them all over the bottle or jar.

Masking tape shapes

83

3. Hold the can at least 12 cm away from the bottle and spray the paint all over it.

4. When the paint is dry, peel off the masking tape to leave the pattern.

●● Canal Boat Toybox

Since the beginning of the canals, boatmen have painted their narrowboat homes with brightly coloured enamelwear. The designs on the enamelwear are traditionally painted using very simple brush strokes. Convert an old tin into a colourful toybox by painting it in the canal boat style.

You will need

Old tin
Gloss paint *or* enamel paint (Deka colour) *or* ceramic à froid (Pebeo)
Paintbrush
White spirit

Instructions

1. Coat the old tin can with black or dark green paint. Leave it to dry. (This could take as long as twenty-four hours).

2. If the lettering still shows through, give the tin another coat of paint.

3. When your background base paint is dry, paint on the design. Paint bright yellow dots for borders.

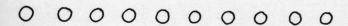

4. Add some daisy patterns by grouping five yellow dots.

85

5. Using white paint, make some long, tapered, curving strokes of different sizes.

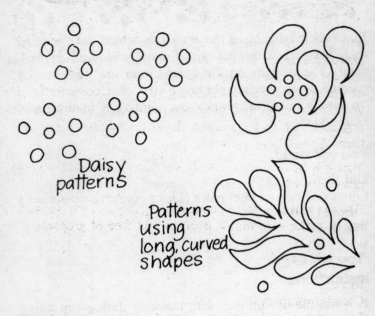

Daisy patterns

Patterns using long, curved shapes

Ideas

Decorate old enamel mugs and saucepans with canal boat art.

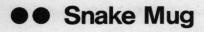

●● Snake Mug

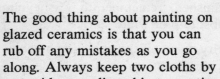

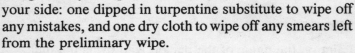

The good thing about painting on glazed ceramics is that you can rub off any mistakes as you go along. Always keep two cloths by your side: one dipped in turpentine substitute to wipe off any mistakes, and one dry cloth to wipe off any smears left from the preliminary wipe.

You will have more control over your painting if you do not overload your brush with paint.

Always wash the item you are going to paint before starting to make sure that it is clean and free of grease.

You will need

Mug
Chinagraph pencil
Selection of paintbrushes (use thick brushes for large
    areas and fine brushes for detailed work)
Solvent-based paints, such as ceramic à froid (Pebeo)
Turpentine substitute
2 cloths
Newspaper
Old saucers *or* lids of jars

Instructions

1. Draw a long, wiggly snake all the way around the mug, using a chinagraph pencil.

2. Paint it a good slimy green, and allow to dry.

3. Decorate with yellow and black dots. Unless you want colours to blend into one another, let each colour of paint become slightly tacky before applying the next one.

4. When you have finished, remember to wash your brush in turpentine substitute or white spirit.

5. When the paint is dry, wipe off the chinagraph pencil marks with turpentine substitute.

Ideas

Paint on the name of the person who owns the mug.

Paint a monkey or a rabbit, or some paw prints leading to a cat.

Or why not try painting a snowman if the mug is not already white.

● ● Birthday Plate

You will need

Plate
Selection of paintbrushes
Ceramic paints, such as ceramic à froid (Pebeo)
Turpentine substitute
cloths
Newspaper
Old saucers *or* lids of jars

Optional extras

Sponge
Masking tape
Scissors
Ruler

Instructions

1. Paint a cake covered in icing and candles.

2. Paint the name of the person whose birthday is being celebrated underneath. Bubble writing is easiest but you might like to try geometric lettering (see p. 32).

Ideas

Try ripped masking tape for random and zig-zag patterns. Cut or rip masking tape and stick it on your plate. Paint the areas which are not covered with tape and leave to dry before lifting off the tape.

89

Copy the markings of leopards, tigers or zebras.

Use a sponge to dab your paint on to a plate. The sponge markings will make their own pattern (see p. 36). Or spatter the plate with paint (see p. 38).

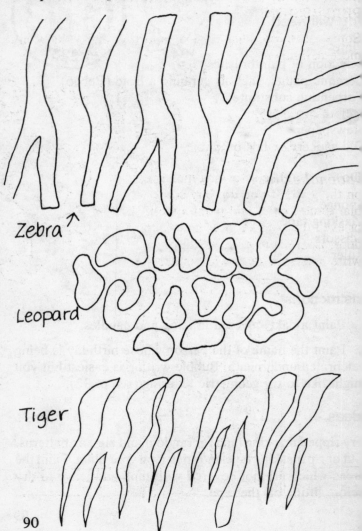

Zebra

Leopard

Tiger

Decorating Walls

Before starting to do anything ASK YOUR PARENTS' PERMISSION!

Some of these ideas are temporary and others are more permanent.

● Graffiti

Do you feel like scrawling messages on the wall? If you do, buy some blackboard paint and paint a wall or even the back of your bedroom door. Leave it to dry, and then write and draw on it with chalks.

OR If you live in a house, ask if you can paint on an out side wall that isn't used often, such as a wall near the dustbins, or the wall of a garage. You may feel simply like spraying graffiti. Or perhaps you could paint something a little more creative, such as a mural.

●● Seaside Mural

As with all the projects in this book plan what you are going to do before you do it! It is important that the things in the foreground, or front, of the picture are bigger than those in the background.

You will need

Newspaper
Scissors
Pencil
Paint and paintbrush
Ruler

Instructions

1. Paint lots of dark blue sea and light blue sky on the wall. Allow to dry.

2. Add fishes, mermaids, shells, boats, even people. If you feel uncertain about how to draw the shapes, cut them out of newspaper first.

3. Stick the shapes on the wall with Blutack. Move them about until they look right, then draw around them.

4. Remove the paper shapes and paint inside the lines you have drawn.

5. Stencil waves near the skirting and ceiling (see p. 50).

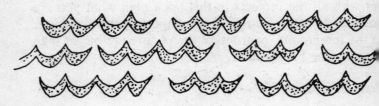

Ideas
Abstract mural:

Cover the whole wall with shapes and patterns.

Cut stencils from newspaper and spray through them.

Rocket room:

On a pale grey wall paint white clouds; paint the ceiling navy blue and spray with gold stars; paint a rocket taking off on the wall.

Fairyland:

Paint a distant castle with many turrets in a sea of clouds with fairies and goblins in the foreground.

Socks, Shoes and Tee-shirts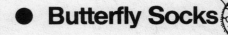

● Butterfly Socks

You will need

Pair of plain socks (white ones are
   best as the colours look clearer
   when painted on white)
Piece of card
Scissors
Fabric felt-tip pens (Pebeo or Pelikan)

Instructions

1. Place your socks on the card and draw around
them.

2. Cut the sock shapes out of the card, and insert the card
in your socks.

Card

3. With the fabric felt-tips draw lots of pretty butterflies and colour them in.

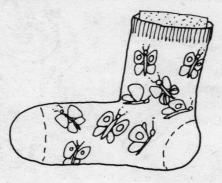

4. Follow the pen makers' instructions for fixing the dye.

Ideas

Try painting fish, strawberries, or flowers for a change.

You could decorate your swimsuit in the same way.

● Leopard Gym Shoes

You will need

Your parents' permission to draw
   on your shoes!
Pair of canvas shoes
Fabric felt-tip pens
Pencil

Instructions

1. Copy the leopard markings on to your shoes with a
pencil.

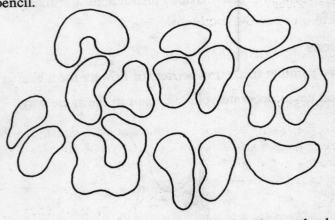

2. Go over the pencil design in fabric felt-tips, and colour
them in.

Ideas

Abstract patterns, ribbons, flowers, and tiger and zebra
stripes all make good shoe decorations.

● Spatter-shirt

If your tee- or sweat shirt is a dark colour, you will need to use opaque fabric paints that sit on the surface of the fabric.

You will need

Tee-shirt *or* sweat shirt
Fabric paints
Newspaper
Paintbrush *or* old toothbrush
Ruler
Saucer for each colour
Jar of water

Instructions

1. Line your tee-shirt, including the sleeves, with newspaper. This is to prevent the paint from seeping through to the other side of the shirt.

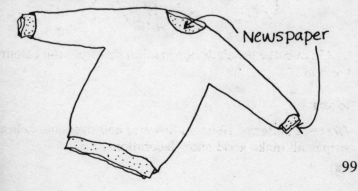

Newspaper

2. Put lots of newspaper down on every surface near where you are working – flicked paint travels a long way!

3. Pour the colour paint you are going to use first on to a saucer.

4. Dip the paintbrush or toothbrush in the paint, so that it is very full of paint.

5. Spatter the tee-shirt with paint by tapping the handle of the brush on top of the ruler (see p. 38), or by holding the toothbrush with the bristles facing downwards and running the ruler along the bristles (see p. 39).

6. When the tee-shirt is dry, turn it inside out and iron on the back of the paint to fix it.

●● Glitter-shirt

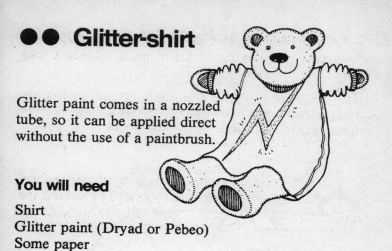

Glitter paint comes in a nozzled tube, so it can be applied direct without the use of a paintbrush.

You will need

Shirt
Glitter paint (Dryad or Pebeo)
Some paper

Instructions

1. Insert the paper between your shirt front and back. Paint on a streak of lightning. You can wash out any mistakes if you do so before fixing the paint with the heat of an iron. Leave to dry.

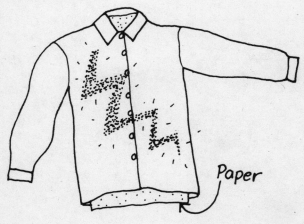

Paper

2. Fix the paint by ironing the underside of your shirt front.

Ideas

Add pretty borders to tee-shirts, cocktail glasses to sweat shirts, and paint flashes on to rollerboots.

●● Puffy-paint Shirt

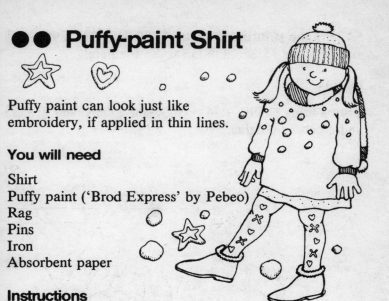

Puffy paint can look just like
embroidery, if applied in thin lines.

You will need

Shirt
Puffy paint ('Brod Express' by Pebeo)
Rag
Pins
Iron
Absorbent paper

Instructions

1. Wash out any finish in your shirt.

2. Shake the tube of paint well before starting, and
remove excess paint from the nozzle with a rag.

3. Pin the shirt on to the absorbent paper.

4. Paint a smiley face on the front. Leave to dry.

5. Turn the shirt inside out and iron with the setting on silk/wool for 15 SECONDS to fix the paint.

Ideas

Try painting clouds, rain or snow on a shirt, and hearts and crosses on tights.

Pillowcases, Scarves and Sweat Shirts ∿

● Galaxy Pillowcase

You will need

Your parents' permission!
A light-coloured cotton, or cotton mixture, pillowcase
Paper
Iron
Pastel dye sticks (Pentel)
Masking tape
Board *or* card

Instructions

1. If your pillowcase is new, wash it to get rid of any starch.

2. Fix the pillowcase to the board or card with masking tape.

3. Copy the design shown on p. 106 with the pastels.

4. Cover the pastelwork with a piece of paper, and press with a hot iron to set the colours.

Ideas

You could draw the letters of your name, or your hero or heroine.

●● Tie-dye Scarf

Tie dye is an ancient technique used to decorate cloth. Parts of the fabric are gathered together and tied, knotted or stitched. The fabric is then dyed. After dyeing, the knotting is removed and the pattern revealed.

You will need

Fabric
Twine, cotton thread, raffia or wool
Cold water dye and fixative (Dylon)

Optional extras

Pebbles
Dried pulses – peas, lentils, beans

Instructions

1. Wash out any starch from the fabric.

2. Either fold or concertina the fabric, and tie knots in it, using the fabric itself or some cotton, raffia or twine.

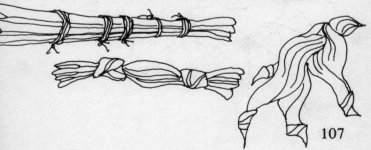

3. Follow instructions on the packet for mixing the dye and fixative.

4. Dip the fabric in the dye.

5. After the length of time stated on the packet remove the fabric from the dye and undo the knots.

6. Hang the cloth to dry.

Ideas

For some different effects try placing pebbles or pulses in the fabric and tying in position.

●● Batik Shirt

Batik is a textile design technique created by the Javanese. They outlined a pattern or symbolic motif on fabric and then poured hot wax along the lines. They then dipped the fabric in a strong colour dye. The dye did not adhere to the wax, so when the fabric was dry and the wax removed the outline design stood out against the strong background colour or colours.

You can create a batik effect by painting a dye-resistant flour and water paste design on to cloth and painting bright-coloured fabric paint or paints on top of the whole surface.

You will need

Pencil
Shirt made of white or light-coloured cloth – 100 per cent cotton
2 cups flour
2 cups water
Fabric paints and paintbrush
Empty washing-up liquid bottle
White or tailors' chalk

Instructions

1. Draw a symmetrical pattern made up of lines on to paper.

2. Wash the shirt to get rid of any 'dressing'.

3. Iron the shirt flat.

4. Copy your design from paper on to the shirt, using the chalk.

5. Mix the flour and paste together to form a paste. If the paste is lumpy, rub it through a sieve.

6. Pour the paste into the washing-up liquid bottle, and replace the lid firmly.

7. Either paint the paste over your chalk design or squeeze the paste out over the lines.

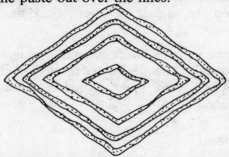

8. Remove any blobs of paste with a blunt knife.

9. Leave the paste to dry. As the paste dries, the shirt will pucker and look as though it has shrunk.

10. When the paste is dry, scrunch the shirt so that the paste cracks.

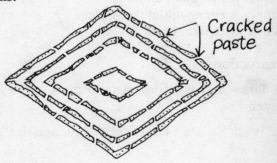

Cracked paste

1. Paint one colour fabric paint all over the shirt. Leave
o dry.

2. Remove the paste with a round-ended knife.

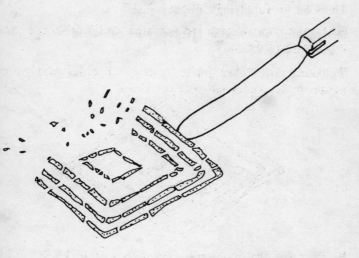

3. Wash the shirt in lukewarm water to remove any
emaining bits of paste.

4. Iron the back of the shirt to fix the paint.

Acknowledgments

Pentel for providing fabric fun pastel dye sticks.

Pebeo for providing Brod Express, glitter paint, and other fabric paints.

Unibond for supplying Copydex glue.

Artists Materials by Ian Hebblewhite, published by Phaidon, £16.95.

Pelikan Fabric Pens.